When You're Shoved from the Right, Look to Your Left

Metaphors of Islamic Humanism

by
Omar Imady, PhD

For information, contact:
MSI Press
784 Northridge PMB293
Salinas, CA 93906

Library of Congress Control Number 2005927125

ISBN 1-933455-05-5

Cover design and front cover photograph
by Carl D. Leaver

Inside illustrations by Amir Abboud

Back cover and inside photographs by Yasir Sakr

Printed in the United States of America

To the Sun
&
her daughters:
Sawsan & Tamara

Omar Imady

Table of Contents

Omar Imady

Acknowledgments

I have long wanted to share the stories contained in this book with readers of English. The project, however, had to wait until the needed inspiration arrived in the form of Dr. Betty Lou Leaver. This book would not have seen the light without her support. Carl Leaver's patience and artistic touch were equally instrumental in bringing this work to publication quality.

Additional thanks are due to my mother, Elaine Rippey Imady, and my friend, Dr. Yasir Sakr.

Omar Imady

Omar Imady

I.
Introduction

Omar Imady

*Bashir Al-Bani
in the White Bridge Mosque — 2005*

What is Islamic Humanism?

There are numerous approaches to humanism, each carrying its own flavor, scent and texture. Islamic humanism is a term used here to denote an approach to humanism that is grounded in Sufism (Islamic spirituality) and articulated by Muslim men and women who are preoccupied, and, indeed, fascinated by the interplay between human spirituality and human sensuality, between what humans plant and what they harvest, and between our thirst for the sky and the sky's thirst for us.

Yet, regardless of how different Islamic humanism may appear from what most of us commonly associate with the idea of humanism, there can be no doubt that the essential idea of humanism, i.e. respect for and admiration of human worth, is just as much a trademark of Islamic humanism as it is a trademark of secular and other types of humanism. Thus, while Sophocles once rhetorically asked, "Is there anything more wonderful on earth, our marvelous planet, than the miracle of man?", the Qur'an, in a markedly similar tone, states:

> *Indeed, We have created the human*
> *in the best possible measure.*

(Q. 95:4)

Bashir Al-Bani, Orator of the Grand Mosque of Damascus

My encounter with Islamic humanism came as a result of a relationship that began during Christmas of 1985. I was then a sophomore at Macalester College, visiting Damascus during my winter vacation. On Christmas day, it occurred to me that a Syrian friend of mine who lived in Los Angeles had asked me to phone his uncle who lived in Damascus and send his regards. My friend's uncle was no common man. Bashir Al-Bani (born in 1911) was once a judge in Syria's Supreme Court. When I met him, he had already retired from his official positions, but he was still a professor of religious studies, an active participant in interfaith dialogue (frequently invited by the Vatican), a master of the Naqish-bandi spiritual order, and the Orator of the Grand Mosque of Damascus. Most important, from my perspective, was the fact that Al-Bani gave three weekly lessons to a small group of students at different mosques in Damascus. His were not lessons on Islamic law, politics, or theology. Rather, as I would later find out, his were lessons that I believe are best described by the term, Islamic humanism.

My phone call to Al-Bani quickly developed into an invitation to visit him at his home, but when I arrived, I found him outside his door. "I'm about to go to a number of churches to say 'Merry Christmas.' You will come with me, won't you?"

"Yes, yes," I replied.

"Yes, yes" were to become the words most commonly used by me in the presence of Al-Bani. I simply could not resist his presence.

Such was my first encounter with Al-Bani, in the old churches of Damascus. He spoke of the Mary he loves and of the Christ he so admires with Orthodox, Catholic and Protestant men of God as though he was completely unaware of how uncommon it is for Muslim religious scholars to have such warm spiritual conversations with their Christian counterparts.

If my friend's intention in asking me to say hello to his uncle was to convince me of giving Sufism a chance, his plan was a grand success. By the time my tour of Damascene churches was over, I had decided that I wanted to be a disciple of Al-Bani.

I recall that on the occasion of my second visit to Al-Bani, which was to mark my first formal lesson, I arrived at his house expecting a lesson in God consciousness, meditation, or any one of those aspects of the spiritual path, but when I sat down, he immediately began speaking about carrots, yes, carrots: the vitamins and nutrients they contain, their beneficial qualities, and so on. Then, he moved on to talk about aluminum. "One must never cook anything in aluminum pots or place juice in plastic containers," he repeated. "Everything, in various degrees, interacts—everything, that is, except for glass."

I nodded frequently, and, after an hour or so, I left his house wondering if I had mistakenly interrupted a ritualized cooking session which Al-Bani was in the habit of conducting. I had been expecting Al-Bani to be entirely preoccupied with matters related to the spirit. Years later I realized that I was indeed right! Al-Bani was focused entirely on matters related to the spirit, but his conception of the spiritual was inclusive of literally everything. It was almost as though Al-Bani had on blue-tinted glasses and, thus, he saw the entire world in a blue shade. In his case, however, they were not blue-tinted, they were "spiritually-tinted." Al-Bani destroyed my artificial classification of the world as belonging to various types of categories: the spiritual, the worldly, the intellectual—and instilled within me the faculty to process life in its entirety through one unified spiritual processor.

But there was much more. At a later stage, I came to appreciate Al-Bani's preoccupation as reflective of his desire to know how the gift of spirituality manifested itself within each one of us. In Al-Bani's mind, nothing provided more spiritual lessons than the way in which the human body operated. Al-Bani could speak for hours about the natural defense mechanisms within the human body, the logic of vaccines and when and why the immune system collapses. In all of this, Al-Bani saw infinite applications on spirituality. There was, in Al-Bani's mind, a spiritual immune system which can be strengthened through vaccination and which can also collapse under certain conditions.

If there is a secret to Al-Bani's spiritual processor, it is no doubt the talent of identifying, exploring, and articulating a metaphor. The metaphor embedded in the idea of cooking with glass was not shared until years after I had replaced, or at least so attempted, every piece of cookware in my home with one made of glass. I did so out of respect to Al-Bani's words and, to a lesser extent, because of my awareness that aluminum, plastic, stainless steel, and many other cookware and food containers did, indeed, interact with food, often producing, in the process, carcinogenic by-products. But when Al-Bani finally shared the metaphor, the poet within me was captivated forever. As we once sat in his home sipping tea in the inner "winter room," as he referred to it, he smiled and said: "Some spiritual paths are just like orange juice in a plastic container. The juice, prior to being placed within the container, is good, but once placed in plastic, a negative interaction takes place, and the result is harmful. Other spiritual paths are like soiled water in a glass container. True, no harmful interaction takes place since glass does not interact, but the soiled water is harmful nevertheless. Orange juice in glass is the spiritual path to which you must devote your life, my child. The content is good, and the form—the container—both preserves its purity and shares its beauty with all."

Al-Bani's delicate sensibility often surprised me. This quality could be seen not only in the way in which he seemed to be always worried about people who were suffering but also in his concern for animals, cats in particular.

For over seven years, I worked as a Program Officer at the Syrian Office of the United Nations Development Program. In this capacity, I was responsible for a number of development projects supported by UNDP in Syria. One day I was asked by Al-Bani about the feasibility of initiating a domestic waste recycling program in Damascus. I said I would investigate it but that environment was not one of the areas that I supervised. Little did I know that Al-Bani's request was destined to be repeated with ever increasing momentum until the question, "What have you done about recycling?", became one that was automatically asked upon my arrival at his home.

"Why?" I finally asked, "are you so concerned about recycling?"

"The cats, of course."

"The cats???"

Al-Bani proceeded to explain to me that he had seen cats eating from the large garbage containers (which are placed at every major street corner in Damascus), and it occurred to him that something must be done to protect them from the pieces of glass that are thrown within the same container. In short, all this was to ensure that cats had a glass-free lunch! Years later separate containers for plastic, glass, and paper were, indeed, placed at road corners in Damascus, but, sadly, it was not because of anything I had succeeded in achieving.

Twenty Nine Metaphors

The stories that follow are, in essence, metaphors of Islamic humanism. More specifically, they are stories which Al-Bani shared with me and other disciples as he attempted to instill within us an admiration of who we are, a thirst for what we can become, and a fear of what we should avoid. Above all, the stories sought to share with us Al-Bani's firm faith in the beauty of the One responsible for us being here.

These stories have never been recorded and were recited from memory, rather than read by Al-Bani to us. Thus, and as is the case with all oral traditions, some of these stories have either known earlier versions or parallels. Al-Bani never claimed authorship. Like all spiritual masters, story tellers, and oral poets, he creates and recreates stories during an organic interaction with his audience. Their originality lies not only in the fact they were shared by a Muslim spiritual master with a Muslim audience within the spatial framework of a mosque but also in the fact that they all are permeated with a distinct spirit, that of Islamic humanism.

While I am completely convinced that I cannot convey through these pages what it is like to sit in the White Bridge Mosque and listen to Al-Bani speak, I do hope that the stories contained in this book will help convey an Islam less spoken of today, an Islam that condemns violence to animals, let alone humans, an Islam that is both deep and reflective, an Islam that is truly humanistic.

Omar Imady
December 2005

Metaphors of Islamic Humanism

Omar Imady

We relate unto you the most beautiful of stories.

(Q. 12:3)

Omar Imady

II.
Metaphors of Islamic Humanism

Omar Imady

The Sheep That Never Lost Hope

Omar Imady

There once was a sheep who dreamed of walking in the very front row of her flock, but each time she tried to move towards the front, she was pushed back by her strong and mighty sisters and brothers.

"Know your place, sheep," they would whisper. "Even the very last row is too much for you."

Day after day the sheep would try to move towards the front row, and day after day she was pushed back with sarcasm.

A dawn arrived when the shepherd, after having directed his flock towards the usual northern pasture field, suddenly stopped and decided he would try out a pasture field to the south which he had heard about from one of his friends. With his rod, he gestured to his flock to turn towards the opposite direction and suddenly the sheep, who had never lost hope, found herself at the very front row.

Omar Imady

For a Few Silver Coins

Omar Imady

O nce a man heard about a place where people worshipped a tree.

"These people are under a delusion. They have replaced the glory of the transcendent God, the secret of all that is alive, with a mere tree? I must save them from this path. I must cut down this tree."

And so the man climbed on his horse and headed toward the tree. When he got there, he picked up his ax and began to strike at it. People ran to him, yelling, "Stop! This is our most sacred tree."

But everyone who tried to push him away from the tree failed. He was simply too strong and too determined. When everyone was about to give up, an old man approached him and said, "Listen, my friend. The truth is that you have severely surprised these people. They are all very devoted to this tree, and they will be very hurt if they see it cut down today. However, if you were to wait just until tomorrow, they will be far more prepared mentally to see their special tree cut down. Meanwhile, here is a bag of silver coins. It's not a bribe, of course. Give it away in charity, or use it for some good purpose. Then come back tomorrow, and you can cut down the tree. I promise it will still be here waiting for you."

The old man's words seemed very convincing. After all, what would a day possibly change? And as for the silver coins, it was true that he could think of many good ways to spend them.

And so he returned to his own town. First, he used a few silver coins to help an old widow he knew, but later he began to use the coins to buy meat, milk, and honey.

"It's OK," he would comfort himself. "I'm simply trying to stay strong and fit so I can perform good deeds."

When the last silver coin was spent, ten days after he had taken them from the old man, he decided he would now return and cut down the tree. When he arrived, he found the old man, along with others, prostrating to the tree.

"Move away!" he screamed. "The time has come for your tree to be cut down."

But no sooner had he said these words than a woman approached him and pushed him to the ground. Surprised, the man stood up and again walked toward the tree. This time a child no older than seven approached him and pushed him to the ground. Suddenly, everyone appeared to be stronger than he, far stronger than he. The faces that only ten days ago were full of fear were now full of contempt.

"Cut down our tree? Who do you think you are to cut down our tree?"

"We'll cut your head off if you try this again!"

But the words of the old man echoed within him the most:

"There is nothing weaker than that which can be stopped with silver!"

Honey & Humility

Omar Imady

After all the animals had been created, many decisions had to be made. One of these decisions involved who would be entrusted with carrying an amazing substance called honey. The animals started to argue with each other, each trying to prove why it should be selected for this special task. The angels arranged for a competition to resolve the dispute.

First, the elephant stepped forward. "I am clearly the most qualified. Not only do I have an enormous belly where all the honey can be kept, but I also have a trunk that is perfectly designed for the task of inserting the honey into containers."

Next came the lion. He roared a few times and then said: "Honey needs to be protected, and who is more qualified to protect it than the king of the jungle?"

Then the horse stepped forward. "Honey," the horse proclaimed, "needs to be transported quickly and reliably. There is no one more qualified for this task than me."

As the animals were arguing their cases, one of the angels noticed that the bee was flying away from the scene. The angel inquired, "Where are you going? Aren't you going to participate in the competition?"

The bee responded, "You must be kidding! How can I possibly participate in such a competition? I am completely and utterly unqualified to carry such an amazing substance. I am nothing but an insignificant insect."

At that very moment, the decision was made. "Honey will be entrusted to the bee because it posses the most important quality of all. Not a large container. Not strength. Not speed. Humility."

Omar Imady

Adam and Musk

Omar Imady

I t is said that when Adam and Eve first arrived on earth, a deer was very eager to meet them. When the deer approached Adam and Eve, they asked her, "Why have you come to meet us?"

"I have come only to be blessed by meeting you," answered the deer.

And so Adam placed his hand over the deer's back, and instantaneously the beautiful scent of musk permeated its fur.

On its way back home, the deer met many animals. They all exclaimed, "What a beautiful scent you carry! Where did you acquire it from?"

The deer would smile and answer, "Adam touched me, and the scent hasn't left me since".

And so before the day was over, numerous animals had gathered around Adam, hoping that they, too, would be touched by his hand and acquire the scent of musk. Although Adam touched them all, they all returned with the same scents with which they had arrived. Only the deer, who wanted nothing else but to be blessed by seeing Adam and Eve, was forever blessed with the gift of musk.

Omar Imady

When You Are Shoved from the Right, Look to Your Left

Omar Imady

A man once went on Hajj (pilgrimage). As he circled the Kaaba (the black cubic structure in Mecca that pilgrims circle seven times during Hajj in worship of the one God), he was suddenly shoved from the right. Wanting to stay focused on his spiritual experience, he ignored this and continued to walk around the cubic structure, like a planet circling a star. Only a few seconds passed before he was once again shoved from the right. This time he looked over his shoulder and politely asked the man standing next to him to stop pushing him, but no sooner had he resumed his walk around the Kaaba than he was once again shoved from the right. This time the man decided that he must put an end to this impolite behavior. He turned to his right and asked the man next to him why he was continuing to shove him, but the man refused to apologize or acknowledge that he had even approached him. Loud voices began to interrupt the serene atmosphere:

"You must stop pushing me!"

"You are deluded! I haven't even touched you!"

A few minutes later, the man felt guilty for allowing himself to be distracted from his spiritual experience.

"Let everyone shove me as much as they wish" he whispered to himself. "I just want to concentrate on emulating the cosmos, circling the Kaaba as the earth circles the sun."

However, as he moved away from the scene, he suddenly noticed that the small leather purse that had been fixed on the left side of his belt was no longer there. While he was obsessed with the man shoving him from the right, another man to his left had been cutting off his purse. How artistically do they divide their roles: one shoves, the other cuts!

What Are You Really Selling?

Omar Imady

A round a hundred years ago in the city of Damascus, all sugar arrived from India. The price of each kilogram was one majidi (an Ottoman currency). Merchants would add expenses and a margin of profit and sell a kilogram for two majidis.

One day a merchant by the name of Tarek began to sell each kilogram of sugar for only one majidi. The sugar merchants were very upset with Tarek, but they decided to ignore him.

"After all," they would comfort each other, "how long can he possibly keep up this ridiculous strategy?"

But months passed by, and Tarek continued to sell a kilogram of sugar for one majidi. The merchants met to discuss the "Tarek Affair." "This has gone beyond any reasonable attempt to gain new customers," they argued. "We simply have to put an end to this."

The merchants decided to invite Tarek for dinner to discuss the matter with him. Tarek arrived and sat with his fellow sugar merchants. A very nice dinner was served and, later, over tea, the merchants proclaimed: "We have locked the door, and you shall not leave until you explain to us how you can possibly continue to sell sugar for no profit at all?"

Tarek smiled, took a sip of his tea, and said: "But I don't sell sugar."

"This is not the time for humor," the merchants said firmly.

"But that is the truth. I really don't sell sugar. Allow me to explain. You have been in my shop; it's just a big room. I have placed the sugar on a big cloth spread out on the floor.

My customers come in, all attracted by the fact that they can buy a kilogram of sugar for only one majidi. So, it is only natural that they want to buy lots of sugar. Where are they going to place all the sugar they decide on buying? Naturally, they need bags. I stand ready to satisfy this need. I have all the bags they may ask for, but my bags are not free. I sell my bags for profit, for lots of profit. But who is going to stop and question the price of my bags when they are getting such a good deal with the price of my sugar? I don't lose on sugar; I simply deliver it for the price for which I purchase it. But when it comes to bags," Tarek smiled again, "that's where I really make a profit. So you see, my friends, I really don't sell sugar. My specialty is bags."

Why the Towel Was Dropped

Omar Imady

Sarmad once decided to go to the public bath. On that particular day, a man who regarded himself as very religious was in charge of scrubbing the backs of customers. Sarmad took his clothes off and wrapped himself in a towel that covered the area from his navel to his knees as required by Islamic jurisprudence from all adult men except when in the presence of their wives.

After Sarmad was done with the steam room, he sat on a wooden bench, waiting for his back to be scrubbed. Moments later the religious man arrived, but no sooner had he entered than he started to scream, "Your knee, your left knee is uncovered! How could you pollute my eyes with such indecency?"

Sarmad looked down and noticed that the towel had moved slightly upward. "Sir, I do apologize, but don't you think you are overreacting?"

"Overreacting? Overreacting? You who have polluted my eyes with the sight of your forbidden flesh are accusing me of overreacting?"

Sarmad was now getting angry, but again he tried to calm the situation. "It was a mistake, an innocent mistake. I have now covered my knee. Would you, please, scrub my back?"

"Scrub your back? You who have clearly abandoned all religion want me to scrub your back?"

Upon hearing this, Sarmad simply lost it. He stood up, smiled, and with a very serious voice said, "You are right, old man. I have abandoned all religion, and here is the proof."

And with these words, Sarmad dropped the towel to the floor, and danced completely naked right in front of the eyes of the religious man.

The Mystery of "Shilabib"

Omar Imady

A man once committed a crime. He was very rich, and he inquired about the best lawyer around.

When the lawyer arrived and examined the case, he said, "Look, the evidence is overwhelming. You will be found guilty in a manner of minutes. There is only one way to get you out of this, but you have to do exactly what I tell you. From now on and until I tell you otherwise, no matter what you are asked, you are to respond by saying, 'Shilabib'."

"Shilabib? What does shilabib mean?"

"Nothing. It's not even a proper word. Now, stop asking me questions, and just follow my instructions."

Later, when the man was asked by the prosecutor what his name was, he responded, "Shilabib."

"Why did you commit this crime?"

"Shilabib."

"Did you act alone?"

"Shilabib."

Are you mentally unstable?"

"Shilabib."

The judge decided that the man was mentally unfit to stand trial and that he should spend some time in a mental institute.

Later, the lawyer arrived to collect his fees. Smiling, he declared, "I told you I would get you out of this. You have to admit that I had a brilliant strategy, but, as I am sure you will understand, brilliant strategies are expensive."

The man just stared at his lawyer, nodded his head, and said, "Shilabib."

"Oh, that's funny. That's really cute. You can stop saying 'shilabib' now, okay?"

"Shilabib."

"Listen, my friend, the case is over. I got you completely out of this mess. Now it's time to pay me."

"Shilabib."

"I am getting tired of this."

"Shilabib."

"I was the idiot who taught you this game, okay."

"Shilabib."

When You Borrow Shoes

Omar Imady

Once a poor man was about to get engaged, but he didn't own a pair of good shoes. On the day when the engagement party was to take place, he asked one of his well-to-do friends if he could borrow a pair of shoes. The friend agreed, brought him the shoes, and accompanied him to the party along with other friends and relatives.

As they walked on the narrow alleys of Damascus, the owner of the shoes would suddenly whisper, "Please, be careful. There is a puddle ahead of you."

Moments later, he would again draw near and say, "Could you walk a bit gentler? The road is somewhat bumpy here."

The poor man's face was crimson with embarrassment, but he had to remain patient until the engagement party was over. How he wished he had never borrowed the shoes and settled for his old ones, instead!

When the party was over, one of his friends who had noticed what had taken place earlier took him by the hand and said, "May that stingy man and his shoes be cursed! On your wedding night you will wear no one's shoes but mine."

And so when the wedding night arrived, the poor man wore the pair of shoes that his other friend had brought him. As they walked towards the bride's home together with friends and relatives, his friend would suddenly proclaim in a loud voice, "Who cares if there is a puddle ahead of us? Step in it! Step in it, my friend! May my shoes be sacrificed for you!"

Moments later, he would again shout, "Step with force my friend. Who cares if the road is bumpy? I don't!"

And later, "By the mercy of my dead mother, you must step into the mud!"

"Khshnakar"

Omar Imady

There once was a man named Samir who always pretended that he was well informed about everything.

"What do you know about the theory of gravity, Samir?"

And Samir would speak on and on about the theory of gravity that he knew nothing about.

"What do you know about Antarctica, Samir?"

And Samir would proceed to describe the tropical forest in Antarctica, which was, of course, located in Southeast Asia.

One day Samir's friends got tired of his boastful claims of knowledge and decided that the best way to silence him forever was to humiliate him in public. So, they invented a word that was a combination of the first letters of their names: Kh from Khalid, Sh from Sharif, N from Nabil, A from Ahmad, K from Karim, A from Ayman and R from Riyad–khshnakar!

They all went to meet Samir at the coffee shop he frequently visited. When he arrived, they gathered around him and one of them said, "Knowledgeable Samir, we have a question only you can answer. We heard someone speak of khshnakar, and we have no idea what it could possibly be."

Samir took his water pipe out of his mouth, blew smoke into the air, and with a very serious expression on his face began to speak, "Khshnakar, my brothers, is a very rare plant. Its original home is in the Sub-Saharan Desert. It has been shown to regenerate the growth of hair, improve sexual performance, and even cure the common cold, but it is funny that you would ask me about khshnakar when only last week I started planting it in my backyard."

The Complaining Servant

Omar Imady

I n the days when servants were bought and sold, there once was a servant who had a very kind master. The master would not eat unless his servant sat and ate with him. When he wanted to rest, he would ask his servant to sit and talk to him. If the servant had nothing to say, the master would share his latest jokes and fill the air with the joyful sound of his laughter. When he purchased a new robe or a turban, he always purchased one just like it for his servant. When he asked his servant to carry a heavy object, he helped him carry it. When he asked him to cook for many people, he would take charge of the most difficult task— finding enough logs for the fire.

Nonetheless, the servant was always complaining. "I am so tired of this master," he could be heard repeating. "Sit with me and eat, sit with me and talk ... do this and do that ... what makes him so sure I want to sit with him? What makes him so confident that I enjoy his company?"

One day the master overheard his servant speak like this and was very hurt, and so he decided he would return him to the servants' market. There the servant was bought by another master. This new master was very different from the previous one. He would never eat with his servants. After he finished eating, the servants ate the leftovers. When his robes and turbans became old and faded, he would give them to his servants to wear. And when he asked his servants to carry out difficult tasks, it was unthinkable for him to help.

With this master, the servant complained day and night. "Eat his leftovers!! Wear his used clothes!! Who does he think he is, the Sultan himself?"

And so the master heard of the complaints of the servant and, once again, the servant found himself in the servants' market. This time, he was purchased by a master who appeared like he never smiled in his life. Not only did this master not feed his servants, not even leftovers, but he didn't provide shelter, either.

A night arrived when the servant stood under the pouring rain, tired, hungry and cold. Suddenly, a man approached him.

"May I be of help in any way?"

The servant looked up and could not believe his eyes. It was his first master who had treated him so kindly.

"Please take me back, Master. I promise I will never take your special treatment for granted again."

And so the master purchased him again. And whenever he wanted to rest, he would ask his servant to sit with him, drink coffee drenched with cardamom, and listen to his latest jokes.

A Bit Farther, Please

Omar Imady

There once was a man who had an old father. The father was very weak and frail. He needed to be cared for constantly. So, the man got tired of his father and decided he would get rid of him.

"Let's go for a ride, Father," the man said.

And he carried his father into the carriage, pulled on the reins, and rode off toward the wilderness outside of town.

After a while, the man reached a place that seemed very deserted. It appeared like a good spot to drop off his father.

"He will die here in a manner of minutes, and I'll be relieved forever of my burden," he said to himself.

But just as he was about to stop, he heard his father say in his quiet frail voice, "Son, a bit farther, please!"

"What?" exclaimed the man.

"A bit farther, please," the father repeated.

"But what difference does it make?"

"You see, years ago my father became old and sick, and I, too, got tired of caring for him, but when I dropped him off, it was a bit farther from here."

Omar Imady

Your Mouth Blew, and Your Hands Tied

Omar Imady

There once was a town that was divided by a wide and deep river. On one side of the river sat a man with a box full of goat skins next to him. This man was an expert at blowing the goat skin and tying it in such a way that it became a perfect float that one could hold onto in swimming from one side of the river to the other. The man was known as the "skin blower," and he would charge a nominal fee for his expertise in blowing and tying.

For those who were better-off, there were small boats available to take them to the other side.

A very stingy and conceited man once wanted to cross the river. Boats, of course, were out of the question since they were far too expensive for his taste, but even the nominal fee which the skin blower charged seemed too high for him.

"Just lend me one of your goat skins, and I will take care of blowing it and tying it," he argued over and over again.

"But it has taken me years of practice to know when to stop blowing and how exactly the skin should be tied," the skin blower answered.

No matter, it was hopeless. The man was too stingy and too conceited to be convinced by the skin blower's words. Finally, the skin blower said, "All right, I will let you borrow one of my skins for free, but you are responsible for the consequences."

"Consequences? What consequences? Saving my precious, hard earned money?" the man whispered to himself as he proceeded to blow the skin and tie it.

However, no sooner had he jumped into the water than the skin began to lose air. The man did not notice at first, but by the time he reached the middle of the river, where the current was at its strongest point, the skin had lost most of its air, and the man, who did not know how to swim, began screaming, "Skin blower, skin blower, the skin you gave me is no good. Come quickly, and help me!"

When the skin blower heard the frantic screams of the man, he stood up and shouted back, "It was your mouth that blew, and your hands that tied!"

Where Do You Keep Your Money?

Omar Imady

A man once arrived in a town. He headed toward the mosque and approached the Imam (prayer leader).

"I need your help, Imam."

"Yes, son, what can I do for you? Do you perhaps have a religious question you need resolved?"

"No, Imam, my problem is different. You see, I have just arrived here, and I am leaving tomorrow morning. And while I have found a place to sleep, I do not feel secure keeping my gold coins with me. I need a place where I can keep these coins overnight without having to worry that they will be stolen while I sleep."

The Imam was quiet for a few seconds and then said: "Imams, my son, are consumed by religion. Protecting gold is not our specialty. However, here is my advice. Tonight after we pray the night prayer together, sit and search with your eyes for the man who continues to pray even after most men and women have departed. This would be the person you can trust with your gold coins."

Both the Imam and the owner of the gold coins were unaware that a man in the mosque had overheard their conversation.

"I will pray until I am about to drop," he said to himself, "and tomorrow I will be rich."

After the night prayer was held, the owner of the gold coins sat, as he was instructed by the Imam, and waited to see who would continue to pray even after most people had left. An hour later, it was clear. Everyone had left except for a man who seemed like he would continue to pray until dawn.

"May I ask you a question?"

The man first acted disturbed for being interrupted but then nodded his head.

"You see, I am searching for a person who could safeguard my gold coins until tomorrow. I was told by the Imam that I should entrust my gold to the man who prayed the most, and I have found none that fit this description better than you."

The man struggled to stop himself from smiling. The fish had caught the bait.

"Yes, it is true that none in this town pray as long as I do. But that's not all. I also fast continuously and read the entire Qur'an once every day."

These words, rather than further comforting the owner of the gold coins, in fact, flustered him.

"I see. Well, I need some time to think this over."

"What are you trying to say? That I am not trustworthy?"

"No, but the Imam said nothing about fasting or reading the Qur'an. He only said that I should find the man who prayed the most."

And the man left the mosque repeating this verse of poetry

I admired his prayers
But feared his fasting.
Had he kept his mouth closed,
He would have walked away with my gold.

The Most Honored Name of God

Omar Imady

W hen a disciple learned that his spiritual master knew the most honored name of God, he became obsessed with the idea of knowing it as well. But the most honored name was a secret that was revealed only to those who had reached a very high stage of spiritual maturity. And so, whenever the disciple brought up this subject with his master, the master would just smile and change the subject. This only enflamed the disciple's obsession. At night, he would lie in bed, thinking about all the amazing things he would do for the world if he only knew the most honored name of God. After all, one of the many special attributes of this name is that when used in a prayer, the prayer always receives a response.

A day arrived when the disciple's curiosity reached its peak. The master realized that changing the subject was no longer appropriate, and so when the disciple once again began pleading with his master to reveal the secret of the name, the master said the following, "This afternoon I want you to go for a walk in the old city. When you come back, we will talk."

The disciple couldn't understand the relationship between knowing the most honored name of God and taking a walk in the old city, but his obsession was so strong that he was willing to do anything that would facilitate access to the secret of the name.

And so, on that very afternoon, the disciple headed toward the old city. When he reached a small alley near the minaret of Christ, he witnessed the following event:

A young man dressed in a clearly very expensive suit bumped into a very old man wearing a green turban and carrying a bag of figs. The old man fell, and his figs scattered on the road. The young man, rather than rushing to help, began shouting, "My new suit! I just hate it when someone touches my new suit! Old people like you should not even be allowed out of their homes!"

As he struggled to save his figs from being stepped upon by passersby, the old man responded in a very sweet voice, "I'm so sorry to upset you. Is there anything I can do to make it up to you?"

However, the old man's voice had no impact on the arrogant young man. "Yes, there is," he said. "Go buy some glasses! Look how wrinkled my jacket has become!" and he pointed to an invisible wrinkle on his jacket.

After recovering from his initial shock, the disciple rushed to help the old man. By then, the young man had disappeared, and the old man was still picking up figs from the road. As the disciple drew near, he heard the old man whisper, "Please forgive him, my Lord; he is so young. Please forgive him; he is so young."

When the sun had nearly disappeared, the disciple's walk was over. He arrived at his master's home, and after they prayed the sunset prayer together, the master said, "Now, tell me, what happened during your walk."

The disciple shared the story of the old man in detail, and when he had finished, the master asked:

"What would you have done had you known the most honored name of God?"

The disciple answered with confidence, "I would have prayed right there and then to have that arrogant young man reduced to dust!"

The master smiled. "So you think the old man was wrong to ask God to forgive the young man?"

"Of course, Master. The old man was weak, and everything he said and did reflected his weakness."

"But, my child, that old man with the green turban is the spiritual master who taught me the most honored name of God!"

Take,
Not Give

Omar Imady

Heavy rain once fell over the city of Damascus. A man walking quickly during the night fell into a deep hole used for storage purposes. People gathered around the hole, and all tried to get the man out.

"Give us your hand," they would shout. "The water is about to reach your head."

But whenever someone would try to speak to him, the man would turn his face in the opposite direction.

"This man must be crazy," they whispered to themselves. "He is about to drown, and yet he resists all of our attempts to help him."

Suddenly, a spiritual master appeared. When he understood what was taking place, he asked everyone to move away.

"What can you possibly do?" they exclaimed. "We are strong young men, and we have been trying to get him out for over an hour. Yet he stubbornly refuses to allow us to help him. He must be trying to commit suicide."

But the spiritual master insisted. "Move away, and I'll have him out in a matter of seconds," he said firmly.

Unconvinced, but out of respect, the men moved away. The spiritual master walked toward the hole, reached his hand out to the man, and with a very loud voice, cried out, "Take it. Take my hand."

The man instantly took hold of the spiritual mater's hand, and the master pulled him out.

"But why did he listen to you and not to us?" the people asked.

"Because this man clearly is afraid of the word, give. Every time you called out "give us your hand," all he could hear was the word, give. I, on the other hand, used the word, take, a word most people love. Take seduced him into trusting me, so he took hold of my hand."

When All Disappears

Omar Imady

There once was a family that lived in a small village. The family owned a goat, a rooster, and a dog. One day the family awoke to find that the goat had died.

"How will we drink milk now?" the husband asked his wife.

The wife had a firm faith in God, and so she answered, "We will drink milk when we are supposed to drink milk."

The next day the family awoke to find that the rooster had died.

"How will we wake up early for prayer?" asked the husband.

The wife answered, "We will wake up when we are supposed to wake up."

The day after that, the family woke up to find that their dog had died.

"Who will alarm us when strangers approach our home?" asked the husband.

The wife answered, "We will be alarmed when we are supposed to be alarmed."

The husband was completely unconvinced, but he loved his wife too much to respond.

When the family awoke the next day, there was a big shock awaiting them. A gang of violent thieves had attacked the village during the night. All the men had been killed and the women and children taken prisoner. Their home was the only one that was left unharmed.

The husband sat next to his wife, unable to understand why the thieves chose not to attack them. The wife held his hand and said, "The thieves didn't choose not to attack us. They simply were not aware of our existence. You see, we didn't have a dog to bark, a rooster to crow, or a goat to bleat — all of the sounds that directed the thieves to homes in the middle of the night. As we were losing our precious animals, we were, in fact, being prepared for an event of which we were unaware. Have faith, my dear husband!"

The Jar That Gave Birth

Omar Imady

Joha had a neighbor who once asked him if he could borrow a jar. Joha hesitated and then, out of sheer embarrassment, asked his wife to produce the smallest jar they owned. He gave it to his neighbor and said, "Please return it as soon as you can."

A few days later the neighbor returned the jar along with another jar.

Surprised, Joha said, "But I only lent you one jar."

"True, but during its stay with us, your jar gave birth."

"Gave birth! Do jars give birth?"

"My dear Joha, of course, they do."

And so Joha returned to his wife, gave her the jars, and shared with her the story of how their jar gave birth. Then Joha walked into their kitchen, found the largest jar they owned, walked out, and knocked on his neighbor's door. "I just thought you might want to borrow another jar."

"How nice of you, Joha. Of course, I do."

A few days passed, and Joha's patience began to run out. Finally, he knocked on his neighbor's door and said, "I just was wondering how my jar was doing."

"Splendidly," the neighbor replied as he quickly shut the door.

Another few days passed, and Joha decided he couldn't wait any longer. "The time has come for me to take back my jar. Would you please hand it over to me, along with its children?"

With a very serious look on his face, his neighbor replied, "I'm very sorry, Joha, but your jar died during delivery."

"Died!?" screamed Joha. "And since when do jars die?"

"Since they started giving birth, of course," the neighbor replied as he quickly shut the door.

Let Go

Omar Imady

There once was a box used to store walnuts. The box had a small circular opening which was used to place the walnuts inside it. A child noticed this box, placed his hand inside it, grabbed three large walnuts, and then tried to pull his hand out. But no matter how much he tried, the child couldn't release his hand. He started to shout, "Help me! Help me!"

The child's sister and two older brothers gathered around him. One of the brothers said, "There is only one solution. We must break the box."

The other brother said, "Our father would be furious if we break the box. There is only one solution. We must cut off his hand."

The sister couldn't believe her ears. "You are both crazy. All you can come up with is breaking boxes and cutting off hands!"

She then whispered a few words in her brother's ear and, seconds later, the child's hand was out unharmed.

"What did you tell him to do?" they asked.

"I told him to let go of the walnuts, of course."

Omar Imady

Stand in Line

Omar Imady

A man who lived a life of greed and desire witnessed a fatal accident. The event shook him to the core, and he decided he would repent and pursue a spiritual path. He searched for a spiritual master, and when he found one, he said, "Tell me, Master, what must I do?"

The master sensed that the most important spiritual disease this man suffered from was vanity. And so he said, "Young man, you must do something that will break your ego."

"Tell me, Master, anything, and I'll do it."

"There's a mosque near the eastern gate of the city. Go today and clean its bathrooms. That would be a good beginning."

And so the man left his master and began to walk towards the mosque. On the way, he would say to himself, "I must be destined to become a saint. Why else would my master ask me to perform such a difficult task? He must be planning to make me his spiritual successor. Why else would he ask me to perform such an unprecedented task?"

When the man finally arrived at the mosque, he rolled his sleeves and walked toward the bathroom area. No sooner had he approached the door than a man stopped him.

"What are you up to?" the man asked.

"I have been chosen to perform a noble and rare task. I have been chosen to clean the bathrooms in this mosque in order to break my inner ego. So, please, move away from my path."

The man blocking the path smiled and said, "Well, stand in line. I am number six. There are five men inside performing that very task!"

Omar Imady

Where Your Heart Lives

Omar Imady

There once was a spiritual master who lived with his disciple in a small shack near the sea. Every morning after performing their meditation and prayers, they would climb into a small boat and spend the day fishing. The fish they caught was their dinner. It was a simple life, and the disciple was convinced that no one alive was more divorced from the love of this world than his spiritual master.

A day arrived when the disciple asked his master for permission to visit his parents. The master granted him permission and said: "On your way back, you will pass by the town where my spiritual master lives. His name is Master Amir, and he lives on top of the hill to the east of the town."

After the disciple had visited his parents, he headed toward the town in which the master of his master lived. He was very eager to meet this man who had so beautifully sculpted his master's heart.

When he arrived at the town, he asked where Master Amir lived, just as his master told him, and he was directed to the house on top of the hill. But when he reached the top of the hill, he was very confused. All he could see was a very beautiful building that almost resembled a small castle.

"There must be a mistake," he said to himself. "How could Master Amir possibly live in a house like this?"

When he knocked the door, a servant dressed in a beautiful robe opened.

"Does Master Amir live here?"

"Yes, yes he does. Please come in, and I will call him."

A few seconds later a man appeared dressed also in a beautiful robe, his head decorated with a beautiful white turban. The disciple stood there, shocked, unable to speak.

A few seconds passed, and then the disciple brought himself to say, "I have been asked by Master Khalid to visit you."

"Oh, yes, Master Khalid. When you return to him, please tell him that it is about time the love of this world departed his heart."

The disciple could hardly believe his ears. He thought to himself, "How can a man who lives in such a beautiful house possibly give my master such advice?"

But, for his master's sake, he decided he would remain respectful. He waved goodbye and walked out.

When he arrived back at the small shack near the sea, he sat with his master and shared with him the tale of his journey, deliberately avoiding the part involving his visit to Master Amir, but that was the only part of the story that Master Khalid was eager to hear about.

"But didn't you visit Master Amir's house?" he asked.

"Yes, I did, Master, and I must say that I was very disappointed. Not only did I find him living in a beautiful house and dressed in a beautiful robe, but also I couldn't believe my ears when I heard him say that it is about time that the love of this world departed from your heart."

Master Khalid's eyes flooded with tears, and he said: "I may live in a shack, my son, wear a torn robe, and eat only fish every day, but my heart remains attached to this world. You see, my son, it is not where your body lives that matters. What is important is where your heart lives."

An Addiction to Weddings

Omar Imady

There once was a man who was addicted to weddings. Not just any weddings. Weddings that were, in essence, an all-women party that followed the formal marriage ceremony. The problem, obviously, was that this man, like all other men, was not invited. So, he would just don a black robe and a black veil and act as though he were one of the bride's female friends.

Time passed, and our friend's addiction got so bad that he couldn't sleep on any night he failed to find a wedding to attend.

A night arrived when his pleasure of attending yet another women's wedding party was interrupted by an unexpected event. A woman suddenly cried out, "I have lost my bracelet, my diamond bracelet!"

The dancing and music were immediately interrupted by very serious discussions about how to solve this theft. Finally, it was agreed that all the women must line up so that each and every one of them could be searched on her way out of the hall. The man stood in line, and underneath his black veil, his face began to sweat. Every few minutes, another search would be over, the line would get smaller, and the man's heart would beat faster. When only one woman was left before his turn came, the man felt he had to do something.

Right there and then he prayed, "Dear God, if you get me out of this, I'll never attend another wedding again."

The very second the man finished his prayer, the woman in charge of searching for the bracelet cried out: "I have found it; I have found it."

Omar Imady

Humiliated for Love

Omar Imady

Shah Naqishband once really missed his teacher who lived in another town, and so, though it was late at night, he decided he would go and see him. The journey took around four hours of walking. When he was halfway there, it began to rain. Then one of his sandals fell apart and the rocky path felt like a razor underneath his foot. It was after dawn when he finally arrived, cold, wet and injured. When he knocked at the door, the master was sitting with other disciples.

"See who it is," the master said to one of his disciples.

"It's your disciple, Shah Naqishband. Should I let him in?"

"No! Tell him we do not allow polluted hearts into this house."

Shah Naqishband heard his master's words, and something in him wanted just to walk away and never come back, but, instead, he placed his head on the door and started repeating to himself, "If you came to be treated nicely, then leave. But if you came because of how much you love and respect your teacher, then wait."

Less than a few minutes passed before the teacher appeared at the door, took Shah Naqishband by the hand, and led him into the house. He sat him next to him and gently began to wipe away the blood from his foot.

"This was your final test, my son. There is no test greater than the willingness to be humiliated for what you love."

Omar Imady

Why the Ship Sank

Omar Imady

There was once a ship owned by a very stern man named Captain Haddad. He tolerated no dissent among his crew. Everyone was expected to work very hard and never complain. The slightest disloyalty was treated in the harshest possible way. No one knows how many crew members were thrown into the sea over the years.

However, there was something very peculiar about Captain Haddad. He had a very old, clumsy cook, who was constantly making mistakes: too much salt, over-cooked vegetables, burned meat, and so forth. Many are the times when he tripped as he was carrying the tray of food to Captain Haddad, but the Captain would only smile and say: "So, my good friend, are we or are we not going to eat today?" Not once did Captain Haddad scream at the old cook. Not once did Captain Haddad even as much as frown in his face.

Captain Haddad's ship was fairly old and had not been repaired in a very long time. In fact, a lot of other ship owners were surprised how this ship managed to remain afloat. So poor was the condition of the ship that ship owners would use it as a metaphor for life against all odds.

The day arrived that Captain Haddad died. His son, Captain Hadeed, as he came to be known, was now in charge. He met with the crew and informed them that he intended to run the ship in accordance with the most modern and innovative methods.

As he spoke, the old cook brought in a large tray of tea, but just as he was about to place it on the table, he lost his balance. The tray, tea, and cups fell to the floor.

At that very moment, Captain Hadeed stood up and said, "Let it be known that my very first decision is to get rid of this clumsy cook that my father should never have tolerated."

With tears flooding his eyes, the cook gathered the broken pieces and walked away. When the ship stopped at a nearby port, the old cook was told to leave. A new cook was brought on board, and the ship sailed on.

On that very night, the ship's engineer knocked on Captain Hadeed's cabin. "Wake up, Captain Hadeed, suddenly our ship is taking in water in at least seven places."

In a matter of minutes, the ship, the crew, and Captain Hadeed faded beneath the waves.

The Angel's Instructions

Omar Imady

There once was a man who was traveling through the desert. The journey took longer than he expected, and soon all his provisions were gone except for a small jug of water and a loaf of bread. An angel carrying water and food was sent with this command, "When he drinks the rest of his water and eats his last loaf of bread, give him the water and food."

And so the angel observed the man from a distance, waiting for him to drink his water and eat his loaf of bread. But the man was so afraid of finishing his supplies and being left with nothing that he simply couldn't bring himself to do so. Whenever he was about to drink or eat, he would say to himself, "But what will happen to me if I were to finish my water or eat my last loaf of bread? I must hold on to them; they are all I have left."

And so he continued to walk, and the angel continued to observe from a distance.

Sometime before sunset, the man collapsed on the sand. In one hand, he held that very last loaf of bread, and in the other, that small jug of water. The angel, still carrying the food and water, kept on observing until it was clear that the man had died.

"How strange are the children of Adam," the angel said as it ascended to the sky.

Omar Imady

Thirsty Dreams

Omar Imady

A woman once wanted to see Mary, the mother of Jesus, in her dreams. And so, upon her next visit to the mosque, she asked the spiritual master what she must do for this to happen. The master smiled and said, "Well, there is no recipe that I know of. You must be thirsty, my child."

"Thirsty?" the woman exclaimed. "But you are a spiritual master. There must be something you can do!"

No matter how many times the master spoke of spiritual thirst, the woman insisted that there must be something he could do. And so, the master finally said, "Tonight before you go to sleep, eat your dinner and place in it five large spoons of salt. Do not drink any water until dawn. The results are guaranteed."

"Ah, ha!" the woman said, "I knew you masters have your special ways. One just has to push you strongly enough."

At home, the woman did just as the master had said. She ate her dinner with five large spoons of salt, didn't drink any water, and went to sleep. No sooner had she closed her eyes than she started having a very strange dream.

First, she dreamt she was near a spring of water. She immersed her entire head into it as though she was attempting to drink it all.

Then, she dreamt she was running after the man who sold fresh orange juice near her home. She was screaming at him, "Come back! I'll buy all of the juice you ever squeezed!"

Then, she saw herself at a wedding ceremony. It was her wedding, and when the groom attempted to give her a ring, she screamed, "I don't want a ring! I want a glass of cold water! I want it now!"

The dream continued carrying her from one image of fluids to another until she finally woke up.

"What kind of dream is this?" she asked herself. "I must go and tell this master that his recipe is completely flawed!"

And so the woman headed to the mosque. When the master saw her, he said, "Tell me, did you see Mary in your dream?"

"Mary! I saw nothing but water, orange juice, lakes, and every liquid known!"

"I told you my child, but you would not listen to me. You need to be thirsty. When you were thirsty for water, all you dreamt of was water. Had you been thirsty for Mary, you would have dreamt of her."

Escaping the Design

Omar Imady

A man who lived in Baghdad once saw the Angel of Death in the market. It was obvious that the Angel of Death was staring at him.

"He must have come to take me," the man said to himself. "I must escape!"

And so the man went quickly to the house of the governor, who was his friend. "You must help me. The Angel of Death is here in Baghdad. He has come to take me."

The governor said, "How would you like me to help you my friend?"

"Send me . . . send me away on your fastest horse to Damascus."

And so the governor ordered that the fastest horse in Baghdad be given to his friend. In only three days, a record speed, the man arrived in Damascus! No sooner had he arrived, however, than he saw the Angel of Death near the eastern gate.

"You actually are here," the angel said.

"What could you possibly mean?"

"Well, I was very surprised to see you in a market in Baghdad because I knew that I was supposed to take your soul three days later in Damascus. How you managed to get here this fast is beyond my comprehension!"

Omar Imady

A Lunch for a Lunch

Omar Imady

There was once a man who lived with his wife and child near a forest. Every morning the man would leave his home and head towards the forest to collect dead branches. Around noon he would sit under the shade of a tree and have his lunch, then head to the market to sell the branches he had collected.

One day as the man sat to eat the lunch his beautiful wife had prepared, a dog appeared who seemed not to have eaten in a long time.

"Come, don't be afraid," the man said to the dog. "I have lunch every day. Today, you have my lunch."

Later, when the man returned to his home after having sold the branches in the market, he found his wife pale and unusually quiet.

"Tell me what is wrong," he said to her.

"Today, after you left, I decided to take our son for a walk. Around noon, as we walked back home to have lunch, a pack of wolves suddenly appeared. I tried to scare them with a stick, but nothing would ward them off. I was sure that they were going to attack us and that we were about to become their lunch. But suddenly and inexplicably, they moved away from us as though ordered to do so by a hidden voice!"

"A lunch for lunch," the man spontaneously replied.

"What do you mean?"

"Today, at the very same time you and our son were surrounded by the hungry wolves, I gave my lunch to a hungry dog. What a small price for the two I love the most!"

Omar Imady

Why the Painting Was Smeared

Omar Imady

Omar Imady

In their stories there was, indeed, a moral for those who have insight.

(Q. 12:111)

Omar Imady

A man stands on a terrace that overlooks a deep valley. He is absorbed by painting the golden clouds of the oncoming sunset. A while later he pauses to assess his progress. He starts walking backward so he can view his painting from a distance. He is unaware that he has reached the very edge of the terrace and that the next step he is about to take will be toward the valley below.

You are standing a few steps away from him. You realize what is going on. Thoughts race through your mind. What shall you do to save him?

If you scream, "Stop, look back," you may scare him and make him lose his balance and fall. If you attempt to take hold of him, both of you may lose your balance and fall. There is only one way to save him: smear his painting.

When he sees your hand moving against his precious work of art, his feet will freeze, and he will move toward you with all his strength. Only then may you take hold of him and explain to him what was about to take place. Yes, you have smeared his painting, but you have also saved his life.

Omar Imady